overcoming
varicose veins

TRIDENT
REFERENCE PUBLISHING

Published by:
Trident Reference Publishing
801 12th Avenue South, Suite 400
Naples, Fl 34102 USA
Phone: + 1 239 649 7077
Email: sales@trident-international.com
Website: www.trident-international.com

Overcoming Varicose Veins
© Trident Reference Publishing

Publisher
Simon St. John Bailey

Editor-in-chief
Isabel Toyos

Art Director
Aline Talavera

Photos
© Trident Reference Publishing, © Getty Images,
© Jupiter Images, © Planstock, © J. Alonso

Includes index
ISBN 1582799725 (hc)
UPC 615269997253 (hc)
ISBN 1582799601 (pbk)
UPC 615269996010 (pbk)

2005 Edition
Printed in USA

overcoming varicose veins

What are varicose veins?

Varicose veins are swollen, irregularly shaped veins that most commonly appear in the legs. Varicose veins in the legs affect about one in five adults, and are more common in women.

Medical experts suspect that varicose veins are hereditary, although other factors such as hormonal fluctuations and excess weight may impinge on their formation.

Varicose veins start when one or more valves fail to close. When valves fail, this allows blood to pool and stretch the veins, further weakening their walls. As the vessels weaken, more and more valves are unable to close properly. The veins become larger and wider over time and begin to appear as lumpy, winding chains underneath the skin.

Different from arteries, veins have valves that make the blood flow toward the heart. A healthy vein has vessels with valves that close to prevent the blood from flowing backward when returning to the heart. In a varicose vein, the vein's wall deteriorates, making the valve incompetent. When the valves stop working blood begins to get stuck, especially when standing. Studies have shown that women are more likely to suffer from varicose veins than men are. Varicose veins affect one in four women in general and one in two women over the age of forty.

CONSEQUENCES
- Slight: pain, discomfort, swelling and tingling sensation.
- Moderate: eczema, skin discoloration, and dermatitis.
- Serious: loss of sensation in the skin, tissue problems and varicose ulcers.
- Severe: blood clots, severely bulged veins.

BLOOD FLOW

In a healthy vein, the valve openings close to prevent the blood flowing backward. In a varicose vein these valves malfunction, not allowing the flow of blood to reverse properly.

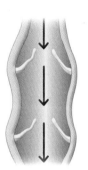

ALERT: BLOOD CLOTS AND RUPTURED VEINS

There are two very serious complications related to varicose veins: blockage (because of blood clots) and ruptured veins. Blood clots are easily noticed, because they tend to be very painful. They have the appearence of tumor like, reddish swellings that don't go down, even when you put your feet up. Ruptured veins are more dangerous, because patients rapidly lose blood. The most sensitive area for ruptured veins is in the ankles. In the case of a ruptured vein, apply pressure to the area to stop the bleeding and go immediately to your doctor's office or hospital.

SYMPTOMS

Blue, swollen, bulging veins or spider veins that are a deep red or purple color are the most visible signs of this ailment. However, sometimes symptoms such as pain and itchiness appear before visible signs of blue veins under the skin. Some people with varicose veins never have any pain or discomfort, just visible symptoms. Varicose veins tend to develop on the inner part of the leg and ankles, especially when the leg is hot. Occasionally, symptoms get worse when varicose veins develop than when they've formed completely.

Most frequent causes

There is no single factor that causes varicose veins; there are usually several factors that may accelerate, if not cause, the development of varicose veins. Although, genetics plays an important role, there are a number of risk factors related to lifestyle and habits.

The most common risk factors include the following:

■ **Heredity.** People with a family history of varicose veins are at greater risk of developing the condition. Studies show that between 65 to 70 percent of children with parents (either on the maternal or paternal side) who suffer from varicose veins develop the same problem.

■ **Hormones.** Varicose veins are six times more common in women than in men. Studies have shown that women are more susceptible to varicose veins during hormonal changes. The circulatory changes occuring during pregnancy also increase risk. Varicose veins may surface for the first time or may worsen during late pregnancy, when the uterus exerts greater pressure on the veins in the legs.

■ **Overweight.** Excess weight puts pressure on surface veins, causing them to weaken. If you are carrying 20 percent excess weight or more you are at risk.

■ **Standing and sitting.** People who have jobs that require them to stand or sit for long periods also are at increased risk. Prolonged standing can weaken the walls of veins, and sitting can aggravate inflamed veins.

■ **Physical problems.** Varicose veins can appear as a result of a defect in the feet (flat foot) or spinal problems.

TYPES OF VARICOSE VEINS

The types vary according to the degree of the problem.

Spider veins or venectasia

These are thin, venous ramifications, either violet or red, and whose importance is basically aesthetic. They are isolated and appear on the legs flat and fine. Over time they tend to spread, increasing in numbers and forming small fan-like or circular branches. They can appear on any part of the leg. Once grouped, they make it more difficult for the blood to circulate, weakening the skin's elasticity and tissue. Venectasia veins are related to hormonal changes (puberty, pregnancy and menopause).

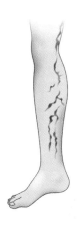

Troncular veins

These affect any of the main leg veins (surface veins). These are the most important types of varicose veins from a medical point of view. They are knots or thick superficial veins that run along the entire leg. If left untreated, they can affect other veins and tissue, due to a lack of normal oxygen flow. In addition to being an aesthetic problem, they can develop blood clots or blocked veins.

Reticular veins

These are small, thin varicose veins which can be found anywhere on the lower extremities. They tend to show up behind the knees or sides of the legs. They form small cords and cause feelings of heaviness, tiredness, and aching.

COMPLICATIONS

Dermatitis, phlebitis and bleeding are some of the possible complications if varicose are left untreated. Dermatitis produces a red skin eruption, with scaling or itchiness skin. It can also cause an area of brown discoloration on the inner part of the leg or above the ankle. A scratch or graze can cause an open wound or ulcer that does not heal. Phlebitis tends to form spontaneously or from a wound. Although this complication is painful, it rarely develops serious problems. The thin-walled varicose vein protrudes just under the skin. Bumping or scratching a large varicose vein may cause severe bleeding. Varicose veins bleed more than healthy ones because of the abnormally high pressure within the damaged vein.

How to treat them

Maintaining your overall fitness, both nutritionally and physically, is most essential to preventing varicose veins from developing. Adopting healthy habits is an important part of treating the discomforts related to varicose veins.

Different from other physical appearance and health problems, varicose veins are not part of the natural aging process. Studies have shown that varicose veins are more common in Western cultures, because of the common habits related to a modern on-the-go lifestyle. It's proven that a sedentary lifestyle and a Western diet (high in fat and refined carbohydrates) are harmful to health. The body doesn't function correctly and varicose veins are just a symptom of a wider range of health problems. Unhealthy habits are the main reason many people develop a range of physical and mental discomforts such as cellulitis, excess weight, back pains and stress. These ailments can be a sign that the body is strained by uncomfortable standing or sitting positions, uncomfortable clothes or ignoring the need to go to the bathroom, for example. Here is a list of tips for changing some of your lifestyle habits to enjoy a healthier body and mind:

■ **Keeping your weight under control.**
When your weight is excessive, it's best to go on a diet to lose weight. This will help to relieve the pressure on surface veins caused by excess weight.

■ **Include more fiber in your diet.** A low-fiber diet can bring on constipation, which can cause varicose veins. It's been proven that pressure on the veins in the rectum when trying to go to the bathroom can transmit to the veins in the legs. Increasing the risk of varicose veins. The best natural way to avoid constipation is to improve your digestion by including foods high in fiber, such as whole grain cereals and fresh fruit and vegetables. Another important resource in preventing constipation is drinking at least eight glasses of water per day.

■ **Avoid high impact aerobics.** High-impact aerobics, jogging, strenuous cycling or any intense activity may increase blood pressure in the legs and accentuate varicose veins.

COMPLEMENTARY THERAPIES

Natural treatments can provide relief from the discomfort of varicose veins, especially when used as complementary therapies to conventional medical treatment. You can also prevent varicose veins with the basic at-home treatment of various alternative remedies. Some of the most effective treatments:

• Yoga.

• Massages and self-massages.

• Reflexology.

• Hydrotherapy.

• Fitotherapy.

• Nutritional therapy.

■ **Use a good shoe.** High heals and flat shoes without any support can complicate blood circulation. It's best to use a shoe that supports your feet. Ideally, your shoe should have a heal of 1^1/2 in/3 to 4 cm.

■ **Changing your position.** Sitting or standing for long periods of time can interfere with normal circulation, increasing the likelihood that varicose veins will develop, and can worsen existing varicosities. While at work, if you have to stay sitting or standing for long periods of time, try to change your position frequently or walk around for a few minutes.

■ **Put up your feet.** To help the blood flow upward, from the veins in the feet to the heart, lift up your feet as high as you can before going to bed. It may be relieving to lie in bed with your feet up against the wall at a 70 to 90 degree angle; stay in this position for 15 to 20 minutes. You may find it soothing to sleep with your feet lifted a few inches from the bed (with a pillow over a wooden board for example), so that your blood flows properly in the legs during the night.

■ **Don't use tight clothing.** Girdles and garter belts, for example, press on the body at key points on the thighs, complicating blood circulation.

■ **Use stockings.** They apply the pressure that helps the blood flow from the ankles upward. This helps overall blood pressure.

■ **Avoid spicy, salty, fatty foods.** These three types of food are harmful for the health and for the vein system in the legs, especially if you are already at risk of varicose veins because of hereditary factors.

■ **Don't expose your legs to direct heat.** Heat affects blood circulation, especially when the veins are weakened. You should avoid placing your legs too close to heaters. Don't use hot wax or expose your legs to the sun at midday.

■ **Avoid birth control pills.** Because of their hormonal content, birth control pills can be a factor in developing varicose veins; it's advised to avoid prolonged use of birth control pills and use other forms of birth control.

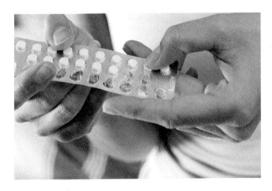

■ **Don't smoke.** Smoking can increase your risk of developing varicose veins, because it leaves toxic residues that affect blood circulation.

■ **Don't cross your legs.** Most circulatory veins and lymphatic ducts are found behind the knees. Sitting with your legs crossed places unnecessary pressure on the legs, making the problem worse.

CORRECT FOOT SUPPORT

When the foot is supported incorrectly (with flat feet for example) the blood doesn't circulate upward, giving a sensation of discomfort and pain in the legs, back and hips, especially when standing for long periods of time. Over time, bad posture due to poor support on the soles of the feet can cause varicose veins. Using corrective sole supports can help prevent pain in the legs and back, as well as preventing varicose veins. However, you need to keep in mind that corrective sole supports are only effective when prescribed by a specialist, after a physical and foot examination. Your doctor can properly diagnose the problem and prescribe a corrective sole support.

Exercises against varicose veins

Swimming, biking, golf, dance and walking are highly recommended in the prevention and arresting of varicose veins. It's best to do these exercises at least three times a week.

➕ The following exercises are recommended to help relieve the discomforts caused by varicose veins. Practicing these exercises 15 minutes a day is enough to give beneficial results.

1. Standing up, with your legs slightly apart, walk on the spot. During this exercise, alternately bend your legs, lifting your ankles as high as you can. You should do this exercise fast, to increase upward blood circulation. Do this exercise for two minutes.

2. *Stand on your toes (both feet simultaneously) and then on the soles of your feet. Continue this movement fast for two minutes.*

RECOMMENDED PHYSICAL EXERCISES

Moderate exercise such as walking, swimming and biking is very beneficial for patients with varicose veins. This type of activity improves blood circulation, without putting a lot of pressure, that can aggravate varicose veins or cause bleeding. When walking always remember to use comfortable shoes with appropiate soles, to cushion the impact produced by your body's weight. While swimming, the water supports the body so that you don't strain joints or muscles. Peddling a bicycle with uniform circular movement stimulates blood circulation. These three exercises also help to keep your weight under control.

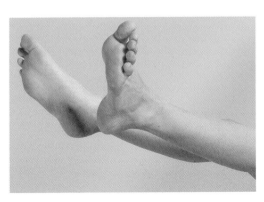

3. *Lying down with both legs stretched out, turn your feet outward and then inward, alternately. Repeat this exercise for one minute.*

4. *Lying down with your legs stretched out on the ground or on your bed, point your toes inward and then outward. Repeat for one minute.*

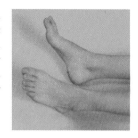
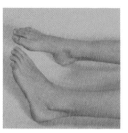

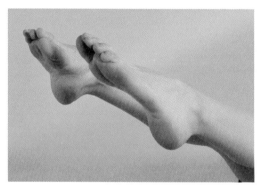

5. *Lying down, with both legs lifted up, continue pointing your toes inward and outward, while rolling your ankles. Continue this exercise for two minutes.*

NECESSARY ACCESSORY

Compression or support stockings or tights are especially recommended for preventing the appearance and spread of varicose veins, because they help the blood flow up to the heart. It's recommended using the stockings or tights daily, especially when you are doing physically active, daily tasks that oblige you to stay standing or sitting for long periods of time. Overall criteria for therapeutic compressive pantyhose include the following:

• The pressure should be distributed from the ankle up to the thigh.
• The heel should be closed (to make sure there is sufficient pressure on the ankle).
• The stockings shouldn't put pressure on your toes.
• Stocking fabric should be a soft, comfortable texture.
• The fabric shouldn't cause you to sweat.
• Use a stocking made with high quality fibers, to avoid allergies.

The therapeutic effect of stockings depends on how tight the pressure of the stocking is, as types of stocking can vary. Your physician should prescribe the grade of pressure of the stocking to ensure an efficient upward flow of blood to your heart.

6. *Sitting down on the edge of the bed, move your legs as if you were peddling a bike for two minutes.*

EXERCISE WITH SUPPORT

A good way to fight gravity with the benefits of compression or support stockings is to practice the following exercises:
• Put on compression or support stockings.
• Next, lie down on your back and lift up your legs, supporting them on the wall.
• Stay in this position for two minutes. This exercise promotes the blood to flow upward to the heart, draining the blood from veins that causes excess swelling in the legs. Repeat this exercise as many times as necessary during the day to provide extra comfort.

7. *Lying down on your back, on the ground or on the edge of your bed, peddle your legs using ample circular movements for two minutes.*

Restoring your harmony

Yoga's stretching and relaxation techniques can be particularly beneficial for varicose veins. Certain positions, such as the Plow and the Candle, promote circulation and the drainage of blood from the legs because the legs are raised above the head.

✚ Except when we lie down to sleep, most of us live straight up, meaning that we are constantly with our heads as the highest point of the body. Yoga is a therapy that aims to attain the unity of mind, body and spirit, through the teaching of body postures, breathing, relaxation, concentration and meditation.

Hatha yoga, the most popular branch of the form, uses many inverted *asanas*. Inverted *asanas* reverse the action of gravity on the body, instead of everything being pulled toward the feet, the orientation shifts toward the head. These exercises encourage a rich supply of blood flow to the brain, nourishing the neurons and flushing out toxins. In these positions, the blood flows toward the heart, helping to prevent varicose veins and relieving discomforts caused by this ailment.

ROCKING CHAIR

This pose is used as a series of movements to be practiced at the beginning of a yoga session to warm up the body. Practicing this pose is recommended for improved blood circulation to your legs. As the name suggests, this *asana* rocks the body, while at the same time it releases tensions making it a good exercise before going to bed.

1. Sit on the floor (or on a padded mat), with your legs bent, leaving the soles of your feet on the floor. Place your hands behind your knees, with your thumbs pointed outward. Keep your chin pressed to your chest to prevent back injuries. Slowly rock backward. Next use your hands to push your legs backward and inhale as your back touches the mat. Remember to keep your chin pressed to your chest. Exhale and return to the first position. Do this rocking motion between 10 to 15 times.

2. Lift up your feet, supporting them with your arms and begin to rock back your body. Rock back and forth five or six times, keeping the legs bent to get the body ready. Inhale and take advantage of the rocking motion to stretch out your legs behind your head. If you can, try to touch the floor with the tips of your toes. Exhale and rock forward, without lifting up your chin. Repeat this movement another 10 or 15 times. Next, lie back down for a minute or two to relax your body.

THE CANDLE

This pose encourages the flow of blood to the heart, helping to improve blood circulation and to prevent varicose veins.

1. Lying down, inhale and extend your arms next to your body, then lift your legs until they form a 90 degree angle. Exhale and when you inhale again, lift up your hips and back and bring your legs over your head.

2. *Bend your arms, supporting your back with your hands, and bring your feet to the floor behind your head. Raise your left leg, stretched (your chin needs to be pressed against your chest, so that your neck doesn't tense up).*

3. *Bring your right leg up, with your toes pointed to the ceiling and stay in this position as long as you can. Next, slowly lower your torso, as you bend your legs, placing each segment of your backbone against the floor as you come down.*

THE RIGHT ANGLE

Encourages correct blood circulation and helps to decongest the legs. There are several variants to this pose, for different level yoga practitioners.

Lying down with your arms stretched out beside your body, lift up your legs to form a 90 degree angle. Stay in this position for two or three minutes and as you become more familiar with the pose, you can increase the time.

If you suffer from high blood pressure it's a good idea to put a pillow or small cushion under your head when you do this posture or *asana*.

Variant 1
If you have trouble keeping your legs up in the air, support them against the wall from your buttocks to your ankles.

Variant 2
Another alternative to this pose is to bend your legs over the seat of a chair to give your legs support; the chair should be at the height of your knees.

PRACTICING BREATHING

The deep-breathing exercises in yoga may further alleviate discomfort by getting more oxygen into the bloodstream. Lie down on your back and place your ankles on the seat of a chair. Breathe slowly and uniformly from your diaphragm and through your nose.

Warning. Don't practice this breathing technique if you have high blood pressure or heart problems, or before consulting your doctor.

THE PLOW

This position favors blood circulation.

1. Begin the position lying on your back, with your legs together, arms by your sides next to your body and palms of your hands pressed to the floor. Bring your chin toward your chest and press your back muscles to the floor. Inhale through your nose and raise your legs up until they are at 90 degree angle with your torso. Exhale, then inhale and bring your hips off the floor, supporting your back with your hands.

2. Without bending your knees, stretch out your legs by bringing them behind your head, until your toes touch the floor. Your arms should stay forward, with the palms of your hands pressed to the floor. Stay in this position breathing slowly and deeply. Next, inhale through your nose and slowly lower your legs while you exhale. Concentrate on how each segment of your backbone presses against the floor as you come down.

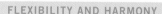

FLEXIBILITY AND HARMONY

Yoga is a discipline designed to improve your flexibility and inner harmony. The exercises use gentle movements without straining your body. When practicing the *asanas* remember not to strain yourself. There is no need to push yourself too far. Remember to use gentle movements and don't push your body into a pose. With time and willpower, you will improve your flexibility and health naturally and become more in tune with your body. It is important to remember to use your body with gentleness, patience and consistency, to prevent side effects like sore muscles or tiredness.

SIDDHASANA

This position favors blood circulation.

Sit on the floor, with your legs in the form of a V and your hands placed on your knees. Bend your right leg, placing the ball of your foot against your left inner thigh. Next, bend your left leg and place the heel near your pubic bone.

THE LOTUS POSE

Sit on the floor with your legs spread out in the form of a V. Clasp hold of your right foot with both hands and bring it high onto the left thigh, up to the groin, if you can. Keep the ball of your right foot pointed upward and your right knee placed on the floor. Next, bring the left foot over the right and place it in the groin. Cup your hands, with the tips of your middle finger and thumb touching. In this *mudra* or hand gesture, the hands have a strong symbolic importance. The union between the fingers symbolizes your connection with universal knowledge and your search for union between your own consciousness and the Universe. The Lotus yoga pose is a perfect meditation posture. You can also place your index finger and thumb together as a sign of your search for harmony and balance.

Steps against varicose veins

Massage is an ancient curing art (cultures have used this technique since 3000 BC). The following exercises may be very useful in preventing and relieving discomforts brought on by varicose veins.

✚ Massage techniques may be a very effective treatment if you suffer from varicose veins, because the practice stimulates proper blood circulation. Massages can be used for surface veins or deep veins, depending on the intensity of the massage. It's important to follow the direction of the flow of blood with the movements of the massage. Always massage upward toward the heart. Don't scratch varicose veins, because ulcers can form, which can further complicate the condition and discomfort. The following steps or "touches" are recommended for those who suffer from varicose veins:

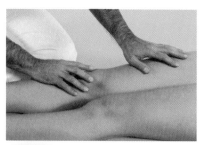

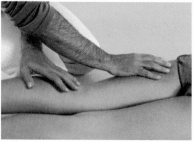

ENERGETIC TOUCHES

Before beginning the massage, you should do this energy cleansing that moves in a downward direction:

Run your open hands over the person receiving the massage, barely touching. Only touch the skin slightly with your fingertips. Moving from the top of the leg to the foot, with long strokes. The hands work alternately; when one hand finishes a downward stroke, the other should continue downward from above it. Repeat this exercise on each leg two or three times. The person should then lie on his or her belly, to receive the energy strokes on the back of the legs.

CALMING TOUCHES

This exercise consists of gently touching the legs with your hands, using only the fingertips in long uni-directional strokes.

Using gentle pressure, run your palms from the feet up to the thighs of the person receiving the massage. The hands should work alternately, so that when a stroke ends the other follows its path. Repeat two or three times, with a good rhythm. Continue with the person lying on his belly, and start the same process again.

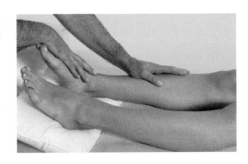

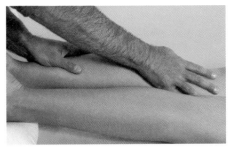

BASIC TIPS

- **Relaxing environment.** The room should be comfortable, with enough space, light and order. The room should be comfortably warm.
- **Correct surface.** If you perform the massage on the ground, it's best to use a padded mat covered with a sheet or large towel.
- **Silence.** You can put soft music in the background, but the massage should be done in silence, without words.

- **Accessories.** You can light candles or a clay aromatherapy pot with a few drops of essential oil for a slight, pleasant aroma (such as lavender or citrus lemon)
- **Fluid and gentle touch.** Your hands warm up quickly during a massage, which can cause tugging of the muscles. We recommend using a cream or neutral oil warmed to body temperature.

RENOVATING YOUR VEINS

This massage consists of ample movements with the palms of the hands and fingers. They should gently but firmly caress the skin using upward movements (toward the heart). The massage helps the body to drain fluids near the skin's surface. The hands help the body to transport the blood with its waste products, so that the area can be nourished with fresh blood.

Gently apply pressure along the innersole of the foot all the way to the inner thigh, trying to rub the entire surface of the leg. Repeat three times; then ask the person receiving the massage to lie on his belly, to complete this massage on the other side of the legs.

WARNING
If you do the massage yourself, remember to never massage directly on varicose veins. Always use gentle pressure.

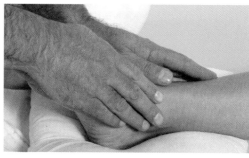

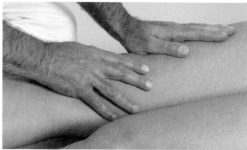

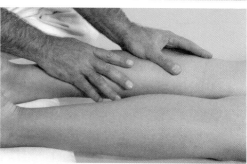

KNEADING WITH YOUR FINGERS

This massage uses your fingertips on the skin.
With your hand cupped and your fingers bent,
each finger should make small, outward and
circular movement. The right hand should move
clock-wise and the left hand counter clock-wise.

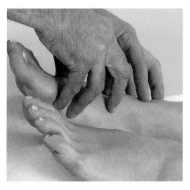

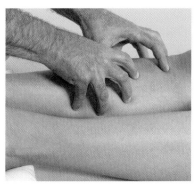

*First, work on the feet. Next with your
hand on each side, work up the feet to
the knee and then massage downward.
Repeat two or three times, covering the
entire leg's surface.*

*Return upward with the massage and
work on the knee.*

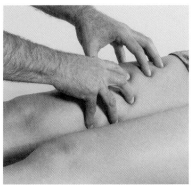

*Next, continue to the groin. Still move
upward and downward with each hand
two or three times on each thigh.*

To end, work down to the foot.

Do-it-yourself blood circulation massages

Do-in massage techniques may help to improve your blood circulation. This complementary therapy is practiced gently and constantly to provide natural relief from discomforts brought on by varicose veins.

✚ *Do-in* self-massage's origins are in ancient Oriental culture. The exercises combine a number of techniques from *shiatsu*, the "physical therapy of touch". *Shiatsu* is similar to acupuncture but without the needles. The technique is based on gentle conscious movements to increase or decrease and finally balance the flow of energy in the body. This is why outlook and attitude are very important for these exercises. It's not effective to simply follow the steps, you need to be receptive to how the massage awakens your senses. Before beginning the massage, it's best to take a relaxing bath.

DAILY ROUTINE

- You should do these massages everyday, especially in the morning.
- Make sure to do them in the following order.
- Remember to only use the necessary energy for the massage. In the beginning, it's normal to tense up the body and the hands. Over time and with practice, you'll learn to do the exercises in an alert but relaxed way.
- If you must sit for long periods of time at work, try repeating these massages again at the end of your work day.

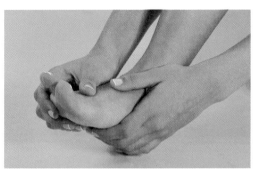

1. Work from your feet, upward. Start with your hands around your right foot.

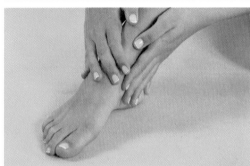

2. Use circular motions on your ankle: one hand at a time, hugging your ankle. You can use oil or cream with gotu kola.

3. Continue with the massage, using both of your hands at the same time, working up your shin and calf.

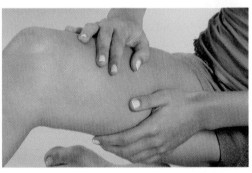

4. On your knee, work the knee cap before the rest of the joint: using one hand at a time, with a gentle, circular motion. Continue working up the thigh, until you reach your inner thigh. If you are more comfortable, you can raise your legs. One hand should move upward, while the other works downward; and then move to the sides of your thigh. Now repeat on the other leg.

Stimulating blood return

When the one-way valves in the veins stop functioning properly, blood stagnates in the veins producing venous insufficiency. There are a number of exercises and massages that can help to relieve varicose veins.

 Arteries carry blood from your heart to the rest of your body tissues. Veins return blood from your body to your heart so the blood can be recirculated. To return blood to your heart, the veins in your legs must work against the natural effect of gravity. This is accomplished with the help of muscle contractions in your lower legs (which act as pumps), and elastic vein walls with tiny one-way valves in the veins. The valves open as blood flows toward your heart and close to stop blood from flowing backward.

To promote the propelling action of this pump, it is recommended working out, walking or biking. Massage techniques on the lower parts of the body may also help. A number of massage techniques is detailed in the following pages.

WALKING

A daily exercise routine can stimulate proper blood circulation and prevent varicose veins from forming. Each step that you take is a new impulse for blood to flow up to your heart.

You can start with a walking workout of 20 minutes a day and progressively increase the amount of time you exercise up to 1 hour.

RELIEVING CARESSES

Foot massages, in addition to helping relaxation can help to soothe your feet and prevent varicose veins, bringing a sense of overall well-being.

Sitting down on a chair, lift up your left foot and place it on your right knee. Make sure you are seated in a comfortable position. Wrap your left hand around this foot and massage its sole with the palm of your right hand, using circular movements. Pay special attention to the arch of your foot. Continue this massage for two or three minutes and then repeat on your right foot.

Another exercise to do at the end of the day: seated on a chair with a foot placed on your knee, wrap your hands around your foot. Use gentle but firm pressure on your ankle toward your toes. When you reach the tiptoes, massage in the other direction. Continue for five minutes and then change feet.

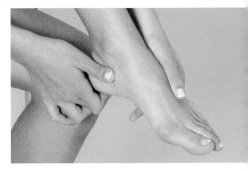

You can also use foot massage accessories on your feet; sit on a chair, place two wooden rods under your feet (use a diameter a little thicker than a broom stick). Move your feet forward and backward, to make the rods spin and massage the soles of your feet. Increase the pressure if you wish. It's normal to feel a bit of discomfort in some spots. Your feet reflect the discomforts and tensions built up in your entire body. (See Decongestive reflexology, on page 32).

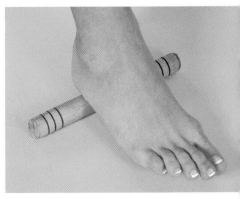

Manual lymphatic drainage

This self-massage is based on manual lymphatic drainage techniques which help to purify the blood and assist its circulation. The massage also tones and shapes the legs.

✚ The lymphatic system is like the blood circulation, the lymph ducts branch throughout the body like the arteries and veins that carry the blood. Except that the lymphatic system carries a colorless liquid called "lymph". The lymphatic system performs essential functions including draining fluid back into the bloodstream from the tissues, filtering and purifying lymph and fighting infections. Manual lymphatic drainage (MLD) is an advanced therapy in which the practitioner uses a range of specialized and gentle rhythmic pumping techniques to move excess fluid and increase the lymph flow. This helps to relieve edema or swollen areas. These massages help to stimulate the effects of lymphatic drainage from the legs. The massages should be gentle, using delicate movements, because excess pressure can cause injuries to the vessels and aggravate your condition.

BENEFITS

- Supports the lymphatic, circulatory and immune systems.
- Helps the body maintain a healthy network of internal vessels.
- Helps remove cellular waste from the body.
- Helps you to relax.
- Helps to soothe swelling.
- Limits cellulitis.

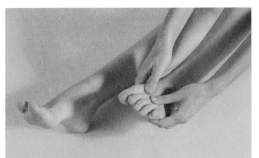

1. Sit down on the floor or on the bed with your legs stretched out. Start with your left foot. Wrap your hands around your toes; your thumbs should meet on the top of your foot and your other fingers should be on the sole of your foot.

2. Use gentle pressure with your fingers, from your toes to your ankle.

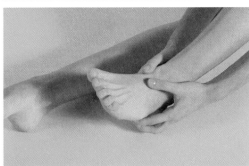

3. Next, without breaking skin contact, work up your calf.

4. When you get to your knee, you can bend your leg to be more comfortable to continue working on your inner thigh. Next, continue the massage on your other leg. You can repeat this massage three times.

Decongestive reflexology

This therapy is based on the principle that there are reflexes in the feet that correspond to the body's organs and glands. Stimulating and applying pressure to the feet may be effective in helping to relieve symptoms of varicose veins.

➕ Reflexology considers that on the feet there are reflex points that can be worked in the treatment of ailments and discomforts. This curative art, dating back thousands of years, uses applied pressure and massages on specific points that correspond to other parts of the body.

TO TREAT VARICOSE VEINS

You should apply finger pressure on three groups of points (A, B and C) to help stimulate blood circulation (see box on page 33). What group you focus on depends on your ailment or the origin of the discomfort. If the group you worked on is the correct area, after a session you should feel relief. You should massage on each point for about fifteen seconds. As in all physical therapies, regular practice is required: two or three times a week, for three to six weeks, to experience beneficial results.

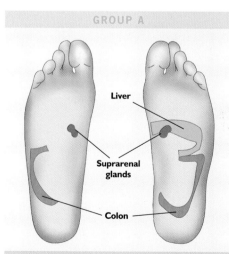

GROUP A

Liver

Suprarenal glands

Colon

WARNING

It's not recommended practicing reflexology on people who are suffering from fever or serious illnesses, are in need of surgery or when the feet are infected with fungus or more serious foot ailments. This treatment is not recommended during pregnancy.

GROUP A
- Colon
- Liver
- Suprarenal glands

GROUP B
- Bladder
- Kidney
- Suprarenal glands
- Spinal column
- Urethra

GROUP C
- Heart
- Large intestine
- Liver
- Lymphatic area in the inner thigh
- Small intestine
- Solar plexus
- Spinal column
- Spleen

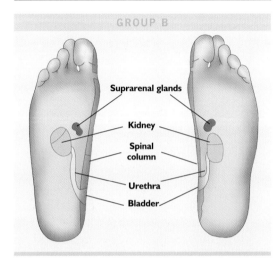

GROUP B

Suprarenal glands
Kidney
Spinal column
Urethra
Bladder

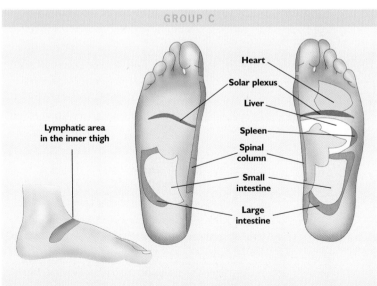

GROUP C

Lymphatic area in the inner thigh

Heart
Solar plexus
Liver
Spleen
Spinal column
Small intestine
Large intestine

Hydrotherapy for spider veins

Hydrotherapy reactivates the body's energy, helps to eliminate toxins and stimulates the blood circulation, in addition to relaxing and harmonizing the body and mind. This is why it is an effective treatment for varicose veins, when the symptoms first appear.

✚ Hydrotherapy uses water's beneficial properties to preserve health and to prevent ailments. Cold water is a particularly beneficial treatment for varicose veins and scarring. This is why it is especially recommended to treat varicose veins in an inceptive state. Cold baths and showers are stimulating and energizing, help to reduce blood flow, inflammation and bruising, and help to constrict blood vessels when they are too dilated.

Another advantage of this therapy is that it is simple. You only need a bathtub, cotton clothes, a plastic bucket and a rubber hose.

WARNING

If you suffer from high blood pressure don't use cold water. Always consult your physician before starting any treatment.

It's important to use this treatment periodically and respect the guidelines indicated for each ailment, because cold water and the time exposed to it can cause significant reactions in the body. We've put together a guide to techniques and applications of cold water to treat varicose veins.

BATH FOR THE LOWER HALF OF THE BODY

You should take this kind of bath in a warm, pleasant room. The water's temperature shouldn't be any lower than 59 °F/15 °C. For people who are very sensitive to the cold, increase the water's temperature. You shouldn't soak in the water for longer than 15 minutes. Introduce your legs into the water very slowly. Don't repeat this treatment at intervals of less than three hours and wait two hours after eating before beginning. After this bath, you should wait at least half an hour before eating food. It's recommended that you do exercises to warm up your body before and after the bath or you can gently massage your legs to stimulate circulation.

■ Application

• Fill the bathtub halfway, so that when you get in and stretch out your legs, the water doesn't go over your belly button.
• You should get into the tub very slowly.
• Stay in the water for 10 seconds.
• Repeat three or four times.
• Afterward, dry off with a cotton towel, with brisk rubs and wrap yourself in a bathrobe.

WARNING
When using cold water hydrotherapy your body should be warmed up before beginning treatment, and you should warm up after treatment. This is why it's important to make sure the bathroom and surrounding rooms are at a comfortable temperature. You shouldn't use this treatment if you suffer from chills or have cold feet.

This bath is not advised for those who suffer from heart diseases. People who suffer from arthritis or urinary tract ailments shouldn't use this therapy. It isn't recommended if you have diarrhea.

AFUSIONS

This therapy uses a hand held showerhead to apply water on painful areas. Water pressure should be moderate.

■ Application

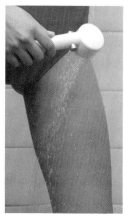

I. Place the showerhead about half a foot away from your left foot. Apply the water moving up from your foot all the way to your waist (over your entire leg and outer thigh.)

2. When you reach your hip, leave the water pressure on this part of your body for about half a minute. Point the shower head so that a trail of water flows down the leg to the feet.

3. Next, work on the inner thigh, moving down the leg to the foot. Repeat this on the other leg.

4. Once you've finished repeat the process on your other leg. Then, on the inner part of the legs.

SCRUBBING

This technique uses a linen cloth, previously soaked in cold water and wrung out. To do a scrubbing you need.

- A bowl with cold water (between 59 to 66 °F/15 to 19 °C, the intensity of the cold determines the body's reaction).
- A thick textured linen cloth, folded several times.
- A cotton blanket to cover the area once you've finished the treatment.

■ Application

Use the linen cloth and rub over the leg in the following order;

- Top of the right foot
- Outer part of the leg
- Hip
- Inner thigh
- Buttocks
- Inner part of the leg
- Sole of the foot

Next cover the right leg with a cotton blanket and continue treatment on your left leg.

RECOMMENDATIONS
This treatment is ideal in the morning. Use this treatment fast, but not with a lot of force. It's important to make sure that the room you are using for the treatment doesn't have any cold drafts.

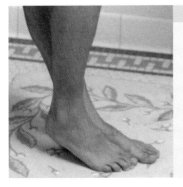

WARNING

Hydrotherapy is not advised for patients suffering from high blood pressure or heart trouble. It's best, if you suffer from any ailment other than varicose veins, to consult a doctor before using this therapy. Also, patients with advanced varicose veins or other related complications should consult a specialist, because cold water can cause other problems.

Home treatments

If you suffer from varicose veins there are a number of simple and accessible complementary treatments that may be beneficial for accompanying regular medical treatment.

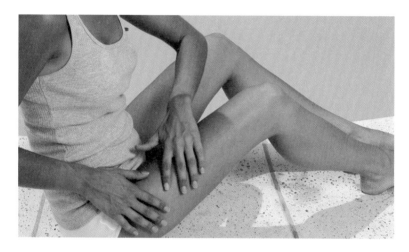

✚ Varicose veins are a sign of a circulatory problem: the blood is stuck in the veins and is not flowing back to the heart properly. This is especially the case for varicose veins in the legs. They can cause pain, tiredness and lack of energy. A simple method to help soothe and prevent varicose veins is to make use of gravity by lifting up your legs. Lie down on a makeshift ottoman by placing two or three pillows on your coach and putting your feet up above hip level. This is recommended whenever your legs are sore and/or tired.

TREATMENT AGAINST TINGLING
To avoid or treat a tingling sensation produced by varicose veins, especially when

it's hot, try to keep your legs and skin cool and hydrated. When you feel tingling or warmth, rinse the area with cool water and then gently massage using a blend off camphor, mint or menthol: dilute a few drops of camphor and mint or menthol oils in almond oil.

Camphor stimulates the skin and acts as an astringent diuretic that stimulates blood circulation. Mint and menthol help to cool the skin down, and have lasting effects. Massaging with these oils added to a base oil not only helps to improve blood circulation to the skin, but also helps to keep the skin hydrated for a quick relief. With continued use, the feeling of heavy, tired legs may lessen.

To increase the oil's cooling effect, keep the oil and other creams in the refrigerator.

EXERCISE
If you have to stay on your feet for prolonged periods of your time, alternate putting your body's weight on your heels and on your toes to stretch out the muscles on the soles of your feet and improve your blood circulation.

MODERATE MOVEMENT

If you have varicose veins, it's important to try and stay off your feet (standing is the worst position for this condition). Try to avoid sitting for hours as well. The best position for your body is to be in moderate motion (without high impact). For example if you are traveling in a car or plane:

- Wrap an elastic cloth around the lower part of your legs (from the toes to the knees).
- If you are traveling by car, make regular stops to walk around and activate the circulation.
- If you are traveling by plane, walk around in the aisle. Try not to sit for too long.

BATHS AND RUBS

These treatments have decongestive effects and are most efficient before going to bed.

Witch hazel

Fill up a tub or bucket with water and soak the legs up to your knees. You can add a witch hazel infusion (1 tablespoon every 4 cups of water). Soak your legs for 15 minutes. Next vigorously dry your legs with a cotton towel.

Grapevine leaves

Boil a cup of grapevine leaves in 4 cups of water for 15 minutes. Next, soak your feet in a bath with alternate temperatures.

GRAPEVINE

All parts of this plant have interesting medicinal properties. They are also abundant in flavonoids and the pigments that have a protective action on the blood capillaries. This is one of the most effective herbal remedies for vein ailments.

- For the first 5 to 10 minutes; soak your feet in a bucket with a hot infusion of grapevines leaves. Continue with another bucket filled with cold water for 10 seconds.
- Change temperatures 3 or 4 times, always starting with hot water and ending with cold water.
- Afterward, massage your legs in an upward direction. Finish by resting with your legs elevated.

OTHER TIPS
- Use a showerhead on your legs every day for 10 minutes and use a massage starting from your ankle all the way up to your knee, to improve blood flow back to the heart.
- Keep the skin hydrated by applying a cream after the shower.

Massages with garlic and lemon mixture

- Cut 6 cloves of garlic in slices and place in a clean jar. Next add the juice of 2 or 3 lemons.
- Add 2 tablespoons of extra virgin oil (its best to use olive or fruit oils) and let sit for 12 hours.
- Before using shake well.
- Put a few drops of the oil on your fingertips and gently massage the sore area, using upward circular motions.
- When you finish the massage (after approximately 15 minutes) cover the area with a long cotton sock.
- Repeat each night at the end of your day.

COMPRESSES AND BANDAGES

Compresses consist of using a cotton or linen cloth (never synthetic fibers) folded several times, soaked in water and wrapped around the affected area.

To treat varicose veins, you should use cold water. You shouldn't apply the compress directly on the skin, first place a thin cloth on the skin to protect it. You can also use another cloth to wrap around the compress to keep it in place.

The following are a few compresses that are useful against problems related to varicose veins.

Lemon

Mix 4 cups of mineral water with 1 teaspoon of fine salt and the juice of 2 lemons. Keep this lotion in the refrigerator and apply as a compress on the varicose area once daily. After elevate your feet for $1/2$ an hour. A variant of this treatment is using vinegar mixed with cold water in equal parts. Apply at night before going to bed.

Parsley

To relieve swollen ankles prepare an infusion with this herb, filtering and then cooling it in the refrigerator. Apply as a compress on the affected area and leave to sit for 20 minutes, keeping the legs raised above hip level.

COLD FENNEL AND LAVENDER COMPRESSES

Fill a bowl with cold water and add 5 drops of fennel essential oil and 5 drops of lavender essential oil. Soak a linen cloth in this mixture and wring it out. Apply as a compress and leave for a few seconds. Repeat this process 5 or 6 times. This treatment is best before going to bed. It has an anti-inflammatory action.

Marigold

Place 1 cup of marigold flowers
in 4 cups of water and allow to
boil for 5 minutes.
Soak gauze with this infusion
and apply to the affected area.

Apple cider vinegar

For heavy, tired legs prepare a
mixture of 2 cups of water with
2 tablespoons of apple cider
vinegar. Apply this lotion to the
legs and then gently wrap them
(without squeezing) with elastic
gauze. Put up your feet
for 20 minutes. Next, take the
bandage off.

Camomile and rose flower

Mix in equal parts camomile and
rose flowers using 1 tablespoon of
each in 1 cup of boiling water; let
steep for 10 minutes. Soak a small
bandage with this preparation and
apply it to the affected area.

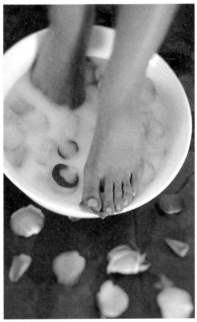

ANCIENT THERAPY

Compresses and bandages have been
adapted and used from the medicines of
ancient cultures. They can be easy to use
and very efficient. In general, compresses
are used as a complementary therapy to
accelerate the curing process. Their
action depends on the ingredients used in
the compress: thermal (for varicose veins
cold is recommended), chemical (herbs,
clay), extracting (mustard) or physical (to
adsorb toxins).

SPECIAL COMPRESS POULTICES

Cataplasms are special paste preparations that are applied with a linen cloth or directly on the skin. You can use a number of different earth elements such as clay or volcanic mud, medicinal plants (cabbage leaves, mustard seed) or other animal products (bees wax).

Clay with onion juice

- Mix medicinal clay with juice extracted from raw onions.
- Apply at night as a cataplasm directly on the skin.
- Cover with a tight fabric or linen cloth.
- Leave on all night as you sleep.
- In the morning remove the cataplasm and clean the skin, rubbing with $1/2$ lemon. You should rub firmly upward but gently downward.

Mustard cataplasms

This treatment helps to stimulate circulation. Mix 3 oz/90 g of ground mustard seeds mixed with hot water to form a thick paste. Spread over a piece of fabric. This treatment shouldn't be applied directly on the skin your are

IRRITATING ACTION

Mustard seed tends to have an irritating action. If you leave on the skin for prolonged periods of time, it can irritate the skin and give a burning sensation. The body defends itself by sending a lot of blood to the area, increasing blood circulation which has a detoxifying effect. The application should be left on the skin for a very brief period of time, to avoid the irritation turning into a sore.

treating. First place a wet gauze on your skin to avoid the paste sticking to it. Then apply the cataplasm and take off some minutes afterward. To relieve reddening we recommend applying olive oil to the skin.

Cabbage

Cabbage has anti-inflammatory properties. To avoid tired, heavy legs cover them with cabbage leaves soaked in water. You should use a cotton fabric. Leave to act for $1/2$ hour.

Oatmeal and yogurt

To clear up blue marks on the legs, prepare a paste with the following ingredients: 1 tablespoon of oatmeal flour, 1 tablespoon of yogurt and 1 tablespoon of wheat germ oil. Mix all the ingredients together and apply on the discolored area. Leave on for 20 minutes and rinse off with water. You should repeat up to 3 times a day.

Cacao butter and wheat germ oil

Mix in equal parts these two fatty elements and apply to the affected area. Leave on for $1/2$ hour and then rinse off with tepid water.

CHESTNUT INFUSION

Chestnut helps to support the veins and blood vessels. This decoction made from the dry nut is easy and fast to prepare. It helps to treat blood circulation problems, and among those, pains related to varicose veins.

• Boil $1/2$ glass of water and 1 tablespoon of chestnuts for 3 minutes.
• Let steep for 5 minutes and filter.
• Sweeten with brown sugar, honey or molasses (not refined sugar) and add lemon juice.
• For the first 10 days drink this infusion 3 times a day before meals. After 10 straight days, twice daily before meals. Then cut down to 1 cup a day.
• Repeat this cycle for 1 month.
• If your pain doesn't improve you can continue drinking this infusion.

Natural relief

Humans have used plants for their therapeutic properties since ancient times, as well as essential oils, made with herbs. These herbs and oils are for topical use and can help in the treatment of varicose veins.

✚ The medicinal plants recommended for the prevention and relief of varicose veins have two groups of characteristics: polyphenols and saponins. The polyphenols are subdivided into two groups, flavonoids and bioflavonoids that are powerful antioxidants found in herbs such as ginkgo.

Saponins, which support the circulatory system, are found in horse chestnuts, butcher's broom and *gotu kola*. The plant species included in the following pages are especially recommended for treating varicose veins. Some can be found fresh or dried, while others come in capsules, tablets or in powder form.

Pasque flower
(Anemonae pulsatilla)

- **Parts used.** The stems, leaves and dried flowers are used to make ointments by the process of maceration.
- This plant grows in humid forests; because of its large flowers it is also grown in many gardens.
- Pasque flower is a very effective sedative, especially to calm pain. Traditionally, this curative plant has been used as an ointment, prepared by fermenting in alcohol or vinegar.
- **Warning.** The fresh plant can be very toxic, but it becomes non-toxic when the plant is dried.

> **NOTE**
> You should always consult your physician before starting any herbal treatment.

Horse chestnut
(Aesculus hippocastanum)

• **Parts used.** The fruits and bark. The nut from this tree has a shell with one to three seeds insides, known as horse chestnuts.

• Minerals, sugar, starch and oils extracted from the seeds are a source of a saponin known as aescin, which has been shown to promote blood circulation. This plant possesses anti-hemorrhage, anti-inflammatory and anti-hemorrhoidal properties. Horse chestnuts are rich in vitamin P, which makes the hair more resistant and less permeable.

• It is also used for the treatment of varicose veins and inflammatory disorders of the legs. Horse chestnut is beneficial in the treatment of chronic venous insufficiency, edema, hemorrhoids, sprains and varicose veins. It is used externally as an anti-inflammatory.

• **Warning.** Do not use it if you are pregnant or breast-feeding. Do not use on children. In high doses it can cause nausea and diarrhea. It can also cause drowsiness.

ESSENTIAL OILS FROM A TO Z

CAMOMILE

Sedative and relaxing, this oil is highly recommended for the treatment of varicose veins. It helps to relieve redness and bruising on the legs. There are many varieties of camomile, but we recommend Roman camomile for home remedies. This oil can be combined with lavender and orange.

Safety. Do not use during the first three months of pregnancy.

EUCALYPTUS

This essential oil is refreshing and decongestive, it is recommended for treatment of varicose veins. It has a fresh, intense and penetrating aroma. Combine with lavender, lemon and lemon balm.

Safety. Do not use it if you suffer from high blood pressure or in cases of epilepsy. It is best to always use this oil diluted.

WARNING

Essential oils are for external use **only**, they should **never** be ingested. Keep stored away from children and keep away from your eyes.

Gotu kola
(Centella asiatica)

- **Parts used.** The leaves are used in a decoction or tincture for internal or external use.
  - This is an ancient plant native to India and grown in other tropical countries such as Pakistan, Sri Lanka, Madagascar, South Africa and also in parts of Western Europe.
  - The plant has antioxidant powers, giving it a strong purifying and detoxifying action. It fights against scars due to its rejuvenating effects on the skin. It improves the flow of blood while strengthening the veins and capillaries. It has been used successfully to treat phlebitis, leg cramps, and abnormal tingling of the extremities.
- **Warning.** Do not take it if you are pregnant or breast-feeding. Avoid this herb if you have kidney or liver problems. If you suffer from gastritis or ulcers you should avoid taking *gotu kola*, because saponins can cause gastric irritation. This herb can cause slight drowsiness, it's advised to avoid driving heavy machinery after taking it. Very high doses can cause nausea.

PURIFYING TISANE

Place 4 cups of water in a small pot with a cover and place on the stove. When it is at boiling point, add 2 tablespoons of dried gotu kola leaves. Cover the pot and let boil for 5 more minutes. Remove from the flame. Let sit for another 5 minutes and then drain. Drink 1 cup of this tisane before a meal (this recipe can be used during the course of the day). Continue this treatment for at least 3 weeks. For topical use, mix with marigold cream, adding 30 drops of this liquid to 1 tablespoon of marigold cream.

Cypress

(Cupressus sempervirens)

• **Parts used.** The pine cones; the leaves and tender branches are also used.

• This tree is considered sacred by numerous cultures, for its long life and deep green color. It is also called "the tree of life"

• This treatment helps to protect the capillaries and acts against hemorrhoids. The plant is rich in bioflavonoids, which are the principal active ingredients (in particular tannins) that help to soothe dilated veins. It is used for the treatment of varicose veins, venous ulcers and edemas (swollen ankles and legs).

• **Warning.** Do not take this herb during pregnancy or if you are breast-feeding.

FENNEL

This is a cleansing oil that helps to eliminate toxins. It has a very fresh and herbal aroma.

Safety. Do not use during pregnancy or if you suffer from epilepsy. We recommend alternating with other oils.

GERANIUM

It is balancing: stimulating and a sedative at the same time. Thanks to its diuretic properties it helps to relieve water retention and aids in the treatment of edemas. It cleans the skin and stimulates blood circulation to the skin. Blend with bergamot, jasmine, lavender, mandarin, camomile, rose, rosemary, sandalwood and basil.

Safety. Do not use during pregnancy.

Ginkgo
(Ginkgo biloba)

- **Parts used.** The leaves are used internally (in extracts, tablets and infusions) and externally (compresses and cataplasms on affected areas).
- Native to China, this tree is legendary, its medical use in China has been traced back at least 5,000 years.
- Its principle active ingredients (flavonoids, ginkgo flavones and terpen lactons) are powerful antioxidants that block the toxicity of free radicals. Ginkgo increases circulation to both the brain and extremities of the body. This plant regulates the tone and elasticity of blood vessels. In other words, it makes circulation more efficient. This improvement in circulation efficiency extends to both large vessels (arteries) and smaller vessels (capillaries) in the circulatory system.
- Ginkgo is recommended for varicose veins, tired legs and degenerated muscles, peripheral vascular diseases and edemas.
- **Warning.** It's important that you consult your doctor if you are taking other medication for circulatory problems, especially drugs that fight blood clots. In large quantities, ginkgo can provoke adverse reactions.

ANTIOXIDANT INFUSION

Place 1 tablespoon in 1 cup of boiling water. Drink before meals, twice daily.
Important. The leaves that have therapeutic properties are yellowish rather than green.

English ivy
(Hedera helix)

• **Parts used.** The leaves and stems are used in a decoction for baths.

• This plant is a climber and stays green all year long. The winding stem grows quickly, it's usually seen on the sides of buildings or growing up fences. It lives for decades and can survive harsh weather.

• Ivy is used in gardens all over the world to cover walls and the ground, as if it were grass.

• **Warning.** If this plant is used incorrectly it can be toxic. To take advantage of its properties apply a decoction of boiled or macerated leaves (cooled down) on the affected area. The fresh plant can cause dermatitis with prolonged exposure. Do not use during pregnancy.

GRAPEFRUIT

Helps to relieve swelling and tiredness in the legs, it is revitalizing and refreshing. This oil can be used during pregnancy, and is recommended to prevent varicose veins during this stage of life.

Safety. It should be used diluted. Avoid exposure to the sun after use.

LAVENDER

This oil has a clean and floral perfume. It is a versatile and widely used oil; it can be combined with most essential oils. Its pain relieving properties can be used for the treatment of varicose veins. It also stimulates skin rejuvenation, helping to prevent scarring.

Safety. Do not use during the first three months of pregnancy.

Sweet clover herb
(_Meliloto officinalis_)

• **Parts used.** The flowers.

• This herb is high in bioflavonoids which help to protect blood vessels and have a sedative effect. It contains a high amount of coumarin that activates blood circulation in the veins, thins the blood and stimulates lymphatic circulation. Applied externally it has light astringent and anti-inflammatory properties.

• This herb is recommended for the treatment of varicose veins, loose skin, edemas, and hemorrhoids and to prevent thrombosis.

• **Warning.** Do not use this herb if you are taking blood clotting drugs or other medications which prevent bleeding. In high doses, this drug can have a slight narcotic effect accompanied by headache and nausea.

Evening primrose
(_Oenothera biennis_)

• **Parts used.** The entire plant (rhizomes, roots, seeds, flowers and leaves). Used for making decoctions for external compresses or in oil (taken in capsule form) for internal use.

• This plant has been used for centuries by the native Americans as an infusion in hot water to treat wounds and other skin problems.

• Primrose oil contains gamma linolenic acid, a fatty acid that the body converts to a hormone-like substance called prostaglandin E_1 (PGE_1). PGE_1 has anti-inflammatory properties and may also act as a blood thinner and blood vessel dilator.

• **Warning.** High doses can cause gastric discomfort and vertigo. Applied locally, this plant can make the skin feel freshened, but can cause contact dermatitis.

DECOCTION FOR COMPRESSES

Boil 5 tablespoons of primrose root in 4 cups of water, until it reduces to $1/3$ the original volume. Apply as compresses before going to bed.

ESSENTIAL OILS FROM A TO Z

MARJORAM

Its warming, analgesic and sedative nature calms and relieves spasms. It has an herbal, almond like aroma. **Safety.** Do not use during pregnancy.

MYRRH

This oil has a warm and resonating aroma that has a relaxing effect. Many people use this essential oil for meditation. Myrrh tones and relaxes at the same time. It is recommended for treating flaccid, dry or aged skin because of its renovating effects. Blend with geranium, lavender, and tangerine. It doesn't have any side effects.

NEROLI

This oil helps to stimulate cellular regeneration, making it an oil recommended for treating damaged skin. It has a light, floral aroma that has sedative properties. It blends well with other citrus oils and with lavender and eucalyptus. It doesn't have any side effects.

BUTCHER'S BROOM POMADE
Dissolve butcher's broom extract in sweet almond oils, in a proportion of 1 part to 5. Massage on the skin, using upward motions.

Butcher's broom
(Ruscus aculeatus)

• **Parts used.** The stems, rhizome and brush-like leaves are used. Mostly the rhizomes are used in infusions, decoction, tinctures and extracts for internal and external use.

• Butcher's broom is a spiny, small-leafed evergreen bush native to the Mediterranean region and to northwest Europe. It is a member of the lily family and is similar to asparagus in many ways.

• Recent pharmacological findings indicate the vasoconstrictive and anti-inflammatory properties of butcher's broom. The saponins it contains constrict the veins and decrease the permeability of capillaries.

• This herb is recommended for the treatment of varicose veins and edemas. It might also help the skin to recuperate after phlebitis. Also used in the treatment of hemorrhoids and brittle hair. It is recommended for internal use to prevent water retention. It is also used in cases of overweight and cellulitis.

• **Warning.** If you have high blood pressure, heart palpitations or moderate to serious kidney problems, use butcher's broom only under the guidance of your physician. This herb can provoke gastric intolerance.

Japanese pagoda tree
(Sophora japonica)

• **Parts used.** The flowers; sometimes the leaves and dried bark in decoctions.

• This large tree is native to China and Japan.

PHYTOTHERAPY

Plants and their extracts can be used in different ways. Some of these are:

- **Oils.** *Prepared by macerating the dried plant or its roots with an aqual quantity of oil (almond, walnut, etc).*

- **Extracts.** *This is the substance obtained when a dilution of the plant, in water or alcohol, has been partially evaporated, leaving a strong concentration of the plant's liquid.*

- **Hidrolyzed.** *When the plant is kept in contact with water, whether by maceration, infusion or decoction.*

- **Lotion.** *A liquid preparation, (from either an infusion or a decoction), filtered through muslin. Lotion's are for external use.*

- **Powders.** *Obtained by milling the dried plant (with pestle and mortar or with a grinder) or its parts (roots, flowers, etc).*

- **Tincture.** *The liquid obtained by dissolving the active part of the plant in an appropriate liquid.*

This tree is used for decoration because of its deep green leaves, yellow flowers and ample shade. It is resistant to both cold and hot temperatures.

• This tree's main active ingredient is rutin, a flavonoid that supports circulation. This plant also contains a number of flavonoids that decrease the blood capillaries' permeability and reinforce resistance. The pharmaceutical industry uses rutin from this plant to make a tonic to treat venous problems.

• **Warning.** Do not use during pregnancy or while breast-feeding.

ESSENTIAL OILS FROM A TO Z

ROSE

This oil is especially recommended in the treatment of varicose veins and dried, aging skin. Its sweet and warm aroma has sedative properties that help to restore the body's balance.
Safety. This oil shouldn't be used during pregnancy.

ROSEMARY

Intense and clean aroma that has stimulating properties that can help to stimulate circulation. This oil also possesses diuretic properties that make it ideal for fighting varicose veins.
Safety. Do not use during pregnancy. People with high blood pressure or who suffer from epilepsy shouldn't use this oil.

Food for healthy veins

A poor diet can lead to overweight and constipation, two factors that may complicate varicose veins. However, eating a balanced diet can help to fight this ailment. There are many nutrients, vitamins and minerals that support the circulatory system as well as overall health.

✚ Eating a balanced diet, rich in fruits and vegetables and low in salt and fats is the first step in treating varicose veins. Dieticians recommend eating a plate of **fresh vegetables** before each meal; this helps to reduce your appetite, provides a lot of nutrients, helps digestion and is low in calories. At the same time, fresh vegetables support the breakdown of carbohydrates, fats and sugars in the digestive system. Citrus fruit like **oranges** and **grapefruit**, as well as other fruit such as **currants**, **strawberries** and **raspberries**, are high in vitamin C, vital for collagen. Collagen keeps the walls of the veins resistant and flexible. Essential fatty acids found in **dried fruits** and **nuts**, **seeds** and **bluefish** also support the circulatory system. Lastly, antioxidants –substances

NOTE
You should always consult your doctor before changing your diet.

POSITIVE EFFECTS OF FIBER

There are two main types of fiber, soluble and insoluble fiber. We need both for a healthy body. Soluble fiber dissolves in water and forms a gel in the intestine, making the absorption of glucose more uniform. It helps to prevent constipation and reduces cholesterol levels. Insoluble fiber works like a sponge: it absorbs water, giving the sensation of being full or sated and making the stool softer.

BERRIES

Raspberries, blackberries and blueberries are rich in compounds that may prevent varicose veins or lessen the discomfort they cause. They are all rich in bioflavonoids and anthocyanidins that help to improve the supporting structures of the veins and vascular system. These dark berries are known for their ability to reduce the fragileness of the capillaries, increase the strength of the venous walls, and muscular tone, and impair the breakdown of the supporting structures of the vein.

found in blue berries, for example, help to repair deteriorated tissues.

One of the factors that tend to complicate the problem of varicose veins is constipation. Studies have shown that constipation increases the pressure on the veins in the legs. To avoid this, we recommend including fiber as part of your diet. Fiber is found in vegetables and is the part the body can't digest. It doesn't provide nutrients but it helps to regulate the digestive process. It is found mostly in vegetables and whole cereals (non-processed, whole grains that the seed and shell have). Whole grains are also rich in B group and E vitamins and minerals like calcium, iron and zinc. To complement a fiber rich diet, you should drink at least eight glasses of **water** per day. Water not only helps to keep you hydrated and prevents constipation, it also supports blood circulation and the elimination of toxins.

Supporting vitamins and minerals

To help prevent and fight varicose veins you should eat a diet rich in vitamins and minerals that support the digestive and circulatory systems.

VITAMINS

Vitamin B₃

B complex helps to maintain strong blood vessels and also helps to reduce cholesterol levels and tri-glycosides. Found in **beans**, **nuts**, **dairy products**, **eggs**, **deep green vegetables**, **tomatoes**, **carrots**, **broccoli**, **potatoes**, **liver**, **fish** and **meat**.

Vitamin C

This vitamin is an excellent antioxidant, helping the body to neutralize free radicals. It's important for keeping the body's collagen resistant, an essential protein needed for the growth and repair of blood vessel cells. A lack of vitamin C can cause small veins to break, which worsens the problems of varicose veins. This vitamin is water soluble, it is expelled from the body quickly; vitamin C should be consumed regularly to make sure that the body gets sufficient amounts of it. It is found in many fruits and

REVITALIZING ELIXIR

In a blender process 1 green apple, 1 carrot and 2 cabbage leaves. Add 1 tablespoon of brewer's yeast, mix and drink.

ANTI-OXIDANT JUICE

Place in a blender: 1 carrot, 1 green apple, 1 stalk of celery, 1/2 glass of orange juice and a few ice cubes. Blend and serve. Another option: place 1 peeled, sliced apple in a blender, add the juice of 1 lemon and 1/2 glass of mineral water. Blend and serve.

vegetables, especially in **citrus fruits, fresh kiwi, guava, currants, oranges, tomatoes** and **red peppers**.

Vitamin E

This vitamin is fat soluble; it is stored in fatty tissue, and is not expelled from the body easily. Processed foods make you lose this essential vitamin, a basic component for balanced nutrition. It has many antioxidant properties, helping to prevent the oxidation caused by free radicals, keeping cellular membranes healthy. It also protects against the destruction of vitamin A, selenium, sulfur amino acids and vitamin C. It helps to relieve fatigue. This vitamin improves circulation, reduces susceptibility to varicose veins, relieves pain, and, sometimes, corrects varicosities. Applied internally and externally, this vitamin helps to keep the skin elastic and glowing. It is found

in **vegetable oils** uncooked, **dried fruits** and **nuts**, avocado, **wheat germ**. Also found in **plums, spinach, asparagus, apples, mulberry, banana, tomato** and **carrots**.

Vitamin K

An anti-hemorrhage vitamin that helps the blood to clot, making it very useful for wounds to heal. It is essential for the formation of certain proteins. A deficiency can cause the reduction in the essential proteins needed for the blood to clot, increasing the risks of internal bleeding. It is found in **green vegetables, root vegetables, fruits, seeds. Alfalfa** is one of the foods highest in this vitamin.

HEALING ASPARAGUS

Cut and throw away the bottom tips (the hardest part) of the asparagus. Wash them well and cover with water. Boil until the asparagus are tender and a deep green. You can make a quick dressing with cider vinegar, sunflower oil and lemon.

Vitamin P

This vitamin helps in
the absorption of
vitamin C,
preventing
vitamins from the
destruction caused
by the air. It is great
for its anti-oxidant
powers that help to neutralize
damage caused by free radicals. It also
helps to prevent varicose veins. It is an
anti-hemorrhage vitamin. It is found in
**citrus fruit, cherries, plums, grapes, green
peppers** and **broccoli**.

Folic acid

Folic acid is great for dilating vessels
and for helping the break down and
clearing of homocysteine from the
blood. Found in **sardines, berries,
nuts, lentils, egg yolks, brewer's
yeast, sunflower seeds, wheat germ, soy,
dried fruits** and **nuts, avocado, salmon**
and **brown rice**.

MINERALS

Sulfur

Helps in the synthesis of collagen and quarcetin (found in the skin). It helps to fight free radicals and helps to restore cells. It is found in **garlic** (especially raw garlic), **cabbage**, **onion** and **broccoli**.

Calcium

Plays an important role in supporting the function of the muscles and proper blood circulation. It improves blood clotting. It also helps the body to absorb iron and is vital for the formation of healthy bones and teeth. It is found in many foods such as **milk**, **cheese**, **yogurt**, **sardines**, **wholegrain cereals** and **sesame seeds**.

Zinc

Is an essential element in the formation of the body's cells. It is vital for the health of the skin and hair. It helps your skin to heal faster. It is found in **red meat**, **eggs**, **shellfish**, **beans**, **asparagus**, **dried fruits** and **nuts** and **sunflower seeds**.

RAW GARLIC

The best way to eat raw garlic is to cut a clove in half and take out the whitish green heart that is found in the center. Finely chop or blend in a blender. Mix garlic paste with salt-free cream cheese to eat on top of toasted wholewheat bread.

FORTIFYING DRIED FRUITS AND NUTS

You should include dried fruits and nuts in your daily diet. You can chop nuts (almonds, pecans, hazelnuts) and add them to ground seeds (flax, quinoa or sunflower) to add to a green salad. This mixture, rich in essential fatty acids, can replace oil as part of salad dressings.

Copper

Helps to form hemoglobin, increasing the absorption of iron. It helps your body to oxidize vitamin C to form elastic fibers. It is found in **oatmeal**, **brewer's yeast, banana, mushroom, avocado, spinach**, and **wholewheat**.

Germanium

Helps to detoxify the body, protecting the cells. It increases the flow of oxygen to the cells. It is also known for its anti-oxidant, anti-cancer properties. It is found in many medicinal plants such as **garlic, barley** and **shitake mushrooms**.

AVOCADO FOR YOUR VEINS

Rich in vitamin E, vitamin B_6, potassium, copper and dietary fiber, avocado is highly recommended for varicose veins. However, you should consume avocado in moderation; the fats found in avocados are positive (mono-unsaturated fats, they don't increase cholesterol levels). But this fruit is high in calories.

DETOXIFYING SHITAKES

They are Japanese mushrooms, when eaten fresh they are juicy and have a savory, meaty flavor. The best mushrooms should have a thick head and the underneath should be a rich chocolate color. Dry mushrooms should be soaked in warm water before eating. You can use them in sauces, or serve them with brown rice or sushi.

Selenium

This is an essential mineral that acts as an antioxidant, together with vitamin E. It helps to keep the walls of the blood vessels and veins elastic. It is found in **meat, fish, whole grain cereals**, and **dairy products**. It can also be found in some **vegetables**, depending on the soil used for cultivation.

index

Introducción

Complementary Therapies

Natural Herb Remedies

Healing Foods